How to Build
Special Furniture
and Equipment for
Handicapped Children

How to Build Special Furniture and Equipment for Handicapped Children

Second Printing

By

RUTH B. HOFMANN
O.T.R., B.A., R.N., B.S.

CHARLES C THOMAS • PUBLISHER
Springfield • Illinois • U.S.A.

Published and Distributed Throughout the World by

CHARLES C THOMAS • PUBLISHER

BANNERSTONE HOUSE

301-327 East Lawrence Avenue, Springfield, Illinois, U.S.A.

© *1970 by* CHARLES C THOMAS • PUBLISHER

ISBN 0-398-00854-X

Library of Congress Catalog Card Number: 70-115385

First Printing, 1970
Second Printing, 1975

Printed in the United States of America
RV-1

PREFACE

I have felt that there has long been a need for furniture for handicapped children that was functional and attractive yet simple to construct without expensive woodworking tools and materials. The furniture and equipment shown in this manual have been made with scrap wood in a limited space with comparatively few tools. All the pieces were sturdy enough to withstand much hard use.

I hope that this manual may serve as a guide for those who might have a need to build for a handicapped child.

INTRODUCTION

A prime requisite in building special furniture is proper measurement of the child so that whatever is built will be the desired fit and will accomplish the desired effect.

Do not glue any pieces unless specifically stated, as it makes changes and adjustments difficult.

Use washers with all bolts.

Use liquid plastic or varnish. It protects the wood as well as making it easier to keep clean.

Countersink all screw heads.

Allow for padding when measuring.

Do not use so much foam rubber padding or other padding that it results in a domed effect.

If considerable pressure is exerted on the galvanized iron supports, use a heavier gauge (16 gauge).

Purchase corset hooks and slide buckles for the canvas harness and canvas binder in an orthopedic appliance store.

The important thing to remember in building a standing table is the three-point contact: the buttocks, the knees, and the heels. If a box is used with the standing table, it should be open so that you can see the alignment of the child and can correct any deviations.

If the furniture is to be used in an institution, you need not have a piece of furniture for each child, as the pieces can be adapted to meet the needs of many children that have a similar body build. The standing board can be made with a notched back so that the angle can be adjusted. The table and standing table can be made with adjustable legs and the box that the child stands in can be raised as well. Use hardwood — 3/4" birch plywood — in the construction of the furniture and rez or polyurethane liquid plastic as a protective coating. The table top may be covered with laminated plastic and edged with an aluminum edge molding.

Before buying ready-made furniture for your handicapped child, consider the fact that it is often prohibitive in price and must frequently be modified to meet the needs of your child. By applying a few principles you can build the equipment that your child needs at a fraction of the cost and with a more satisfactory end result.

CONTENTS

How to Build
Special Furniture
and Equipment for
Handicapped Children

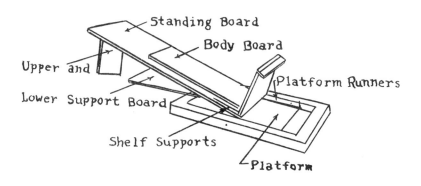

Standing Board

Body Board

Upper and

Platform Runners

Lower Support Board

Shelf Supports

Platform

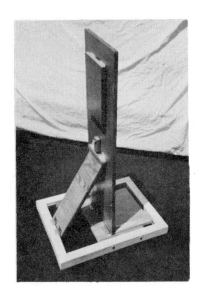

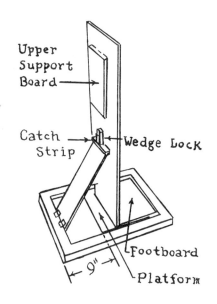

Upper
Support
Board

Catch
Strip

Wedge Lock

9"

Footboard

Platform

STANDING BOARD

For the child who is unable to stand without extensive support. It provides an opportunity for weight bearing, improves balance and circulation.

MATERIALS

Textured plastic material
Rug or rubber rug padding
100C garnet paper
Shellac
Polyurethane liquid plastic
Pine – 1 3/4″ x 1 3/4″
Ply – 3/4″
Hinges – two 1 1/2″, two 2″, two
2 1/2″ light narrow steel butt
Two 3″ light tee hinges
Screw-Guide
Screws #6 flathead – 5/8″, 3/4″,
1 1/4″, 1 1/2″

Shelf supports 6″ x 8″ or 10″ x
12″
Four 2″ angle irons
1/4″ drill
Four 3″ carriage bolts, 1/4″ diam.
One 2″ flat head stove bolt 1/4″
diam.
Six 1/4″ washers
5/8″ tacks
One 1/4″ winged nut
Countersink
Ten 7/8″ furniture glides

If building for a young adult:
Four 4″ heavy tee hinges
Two 2″ heavy gauge steel butt hinges
Screws #9 3/4″.

MEASUREMENT OF CHILD

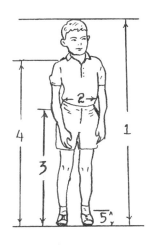

1. Height
2. Width of body – get newspaper pattern for table cut-out
3. Distance from elbow to floor
4. Distance from shoulder to feet
5. Shoe length
6. Newspaper pattern for canvas harness (p. 9)
7. Measurements for knee support (p. 10)

CONSTRUCTION

Use 3/4″ply unless otherwise indicated. Use the Screw-Guide #1465 for #6 screws for all holes as it makes the pilot hole and countersink in one step. Sand pieces with 100C garnet paper as you go. Shellac before tacking on the padding. Use the Polyurethane varnish on surfaces that will receive wear.

Standing Board   Cut 1

Use 3/4″ ply, grain running longways
Width: 12″ , 14″ or whatever is available
Length: add 10″ to height of child

Footboard   Cut 1

Width: same as standing board
Length: add 4″ to shoe measurement

Footboard Strip   Cut 1

Width: 1″ to 1 1/2″
Length: same as footboard
Thickness: 1″ or as much of a tilt that you want
on the standing board

Platform   Cut 1

Width: add 3″ to width of footboard
Length: add 1″ to length of footboard

Platform Runners   Cut 2

Length: the length of
the platform
Height: 1 1/16″

Assembly

Attach the footboard to the standing board using 6″ x 8″ shelf supports and 3/4″ screws. Use the 10″ x 12″ size for older children or for boards over four feet tall. Screw the footboard strip to the front edge of the footboard using two 1 1/2″ screws. Screw up from the bottom. Screw

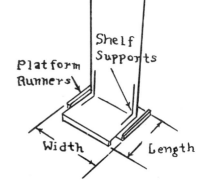

Shelf Supports

Platform Runners

Width

Length

the platform runners on the sides of the platform using two 1 1/4″ screws on each side. Screw up from the bottom.

Screw two 2 1/2″ butt hinges on the back bottom edge of the standing board 1″ in from each side. Use 3/4″ screws. If you are building for a young adult use the 4″ heavy tee hinges and #9 screws.

Center the standing board on the platform 3″ from the back, mark but do not screw hinges to the platform as the standing board is removed when you bolt the frame to the platform.

Frame

Use pine 1 3/4″ x 1 3/4″
> Width: same as platform   Cut 2
> Length: length of platform
>> Plus the overhanding footboard (refer to diagram on page 4)
>> Add 12″
>>> 18″ or more if standing board is over 4′ tall
> Cut 2

Assemble frame using 2″ angle irons in each corner. Put the platform, from which the standing board has been removed, inside the frame 9″ from the back end. Drill 1/4″ holes through the frame and platform runners. Bolt the frame to the platform using four 3″ carriage bolts. Place washers on the bolts before tightening the nuts.

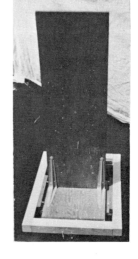

Place the standing board on the platform 3″ from the back and screw the hinges into position using 3/4″ screws. Fasten glides to the under surface of platform, frame and footboard strip.

5

On Back of Standing Board

Lower Support Board   Cut 1

    Width: 8″ to 10″ wide depending on width of
      standing board

    Length: 22″ to 24″ — this varies with the height
      of the standing board. If over 4′ bring your
      support board about half way up.

Catch Strip   Cut 1

    Width: 1″

    Length: the width of the lower support board

Wedge Lock   Cut 1

    Width: 1 1/2″

    Length: 3″

Upper Support Board   Cut 1

    Width: 8″ to 12″ depending on width of standing
      board

    Length: 8″ to 10″

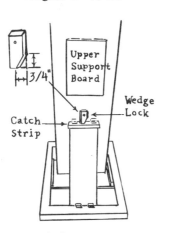

Assembly

    Screw two 3″ light tee hinges on the lower support board 3/4″ in from each side, using 3/4″ screws. For a young adult use two heavy tee hinges and #9 screws. Center the board on the frame and screw into place.

    Catch Strip. Screw two 1 1/2″ hinges 1/2″ in from each side, using 3/4″ screws. Place the catch strip on top of the lower support board as it rests against the standing board. Screw the hinges to the standing board, which will now be stationary.

    Wedge Lock. Cut off the right corner and drill a 1/4″ hole in the center 3/4″ from the top. Center the wedge lock on top of the hinged catch strip — fit snugly. Put the 1/4″ drill through the hole in the wedge lock and drill through the standing board. Put a 2″ flat head 1/4″ diameter stove bolt through the hole from the front side of the standing board — countersink the head. Place a 1/4″ washer on the bolt in front as well as in back of the wedge lock. Use a 1/4″ winged nut to tighten. The wedge lock will hold the catch strip securely against the lower support board so that the standing board will not fall backwards inadvertently.

    Upper Support Board. Screw two 2″ hinges 3/4″ in from each side. For a young adult use a heavier gauge steel hinge rather than the light narrow butt hinge. Turn the board over so that the hinges are out of sight. Mount on the standing board 2 1/2″ from the top or more if desired. This board holds the standing board in an inclined position when the child is being placed on the board. It should be mounted so that it clears the frame and the lower support board.

On Front of Standing Board

Body Board (see picture on page 2)

This board sets the childs' body 3/4" forward so that the child has more freedom in head movement.

    Width: the distance between the shelf supports   Cut 1

    Length: the distance from shoulder to feet

Assembly

Mount on the standing board with the bottom edge resting on the footboard. Screw in from each side using three 1 1/4 " screws. As the child grows the body board can be raised by unscrewing the side screws without removing the harness and padding, and a suitably sized 3/4" padded block inserted to fill in the space.

Pad the body board with rug or rubber padding and cover with textured plastic material. Tack into place with 5/8" tacks.

V-Shaped Headrest

Provides good head support for the child that has minimal head control.

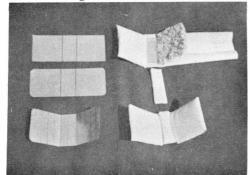

Materials
Tin snips
Rug scraps
1/2 yard plastic material
3/16" metal drill
22 gauge galvanized iron
Two 1 1/2" round head bolts
3/16" diam.
Two 3/16" washers
Round elastic cord
1/2" foam rubber
1 yard denim

Procedure

Cut one piece of galvanized iron 4 1/2" x 11 1/4". Round corners. Drill two holes in the center panel and bend sides forward slightly. Cover the metal side (a), back and front, with rug padding which is cut 3/16" larger than the metal on three sides. Sew padding edges together with string. Repeat on the other side. Cover the entire headrest with plastic material, sewing the tucked in edges with string.

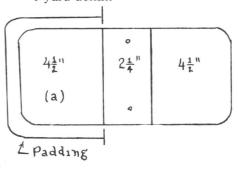

A larger headrest may be needed in some instances. See following pages for instructions.

7

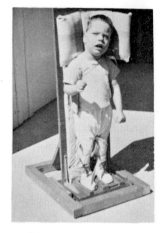

The child may need a larger headrest that will touch his shoulder and be far enough out to prevent him from dropping his head under the headrest.

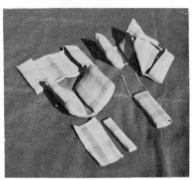
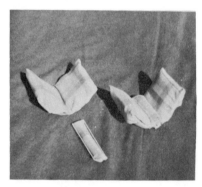

Cut a 6″ x 11 1/4″ piece of galvanized iron and cover it with rug padding. For additional comfort, pad the side (a) section with foam rubber. Refer to the diagram on the preceeding page. Cover with denim. Make a removable cover which can be slipped over the ends of the headrest. Cover a piece of foam rubber the size of the center panel with denim and make a removable cover as well. If you sew a piece of round elastic cord on each side it can be easily placed into position.

Attaching on Standing Board

Center the headrest on the standing board with the upper edge 2″ above the height of the child. This will center the child's head in the headrest. Put the 3/16″ drill through the holes in the center panel and drill the holes into the standing board. Bolt the headrest into position using two 1 1/2″ bolts and washers. Slip the padded plastic or denim covered center section into place, covering the heads of the bolts.

Flat Pad Headrest (pictured on pages 33, 34)

A flat pad is used for a child that has no problem in head control.

Cut a piece of rug padding the width of the body board and 8″ long. Cover with plastic material and place into position – the upper edge 2″ above the height of the child. Use 5/8″ tacks to secure.

Canvas Harness and Knee Support

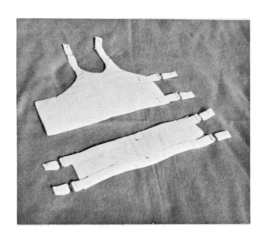

Materials

Light weight canvas
2 yds. 1″ corset webbing
Eight 1″ corset hooks and slide buckles (#7011)
22 gauge galvanized iron
Ten 3/4″ #6 screws
1/8″ metal drill
Ten #6 finishing washers

Harness

Cut and fit a newspaper pattern on the child. The bottom of harness comes to the child's waist. It should not bind at neck or under the arms. The sides touch the surface on which the child is lying. Allow 3″ extra length on the left side. The excess is turned under — it gives you room to place your screws and can be let out as the child grows.

Procedure. Place the pattern on the canvas and cut double thickness.

Cut webbing: 2 strips 6″ long (shoulder straps)
                  2 strips 8″ long (side straps)

Sew the harness leaving one side and the top of the harness shoulder straps open. Turn right side out and press flat. Stitch the side opening. Insert the 6″ webbing strips into each shoulder strap and stitch 1 1/4″ deep. Place the two 8″ strips on the right side 3 1/2″ in from the edge and stitch the end 1 1/4″ deep. The harness can then be tightened when the child is placed on the standing board.

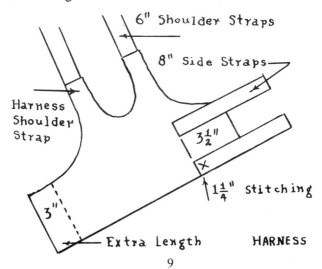

6″ Shoulder Straps

8″ Side Straps

Harness Shoulder Strap

$3\frac{1}{2}″$

$1\frac{1}{4}″$ stitching

3″

Extra Length   HARNESS

9

Knee Support

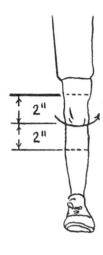

Width: measure 2″ above and below the child's knee

Length: measure around the child's leg at the knee — double this figure and add 3 1/2″. This will give you 1 1/2″ for the space between the knees and 2″ for seams and play.

Procedure. Cut canvas double thickness. Stitch on three sides leaving one end open (1). Turn right side out and press. Fold to mark the center (2). Mark lightly 3/4″ to the left of the center crease, fold and stitch (3). Cut a piece of galvanized iron 1 1/2″ wide and 1/4″ less than the width of the knee support in length. Drill two 1/8″ holes in the metal and round off the sharp edges (4). Insert metal (5) and stitch on the right side of the metal space and the open end of the canvas (6). Pierce, with a compass point, the canvas which covers the holes in the metal spacer.

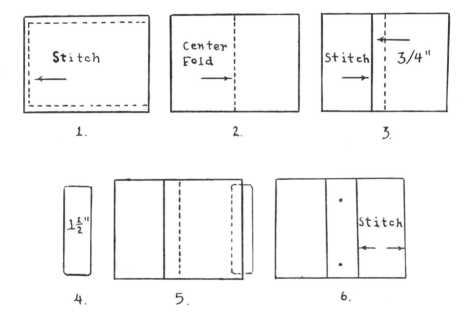

Cut four strips of webbing 8″ long. Place the strips on each side of the canvas knee support 3 1/2″ in from the edge and stitch the end 1 1/4″ deep.

Inserting the Webbing in the Hooks.

Cut 8 strips of webbing 3 1/2" long. Center a hook on each strip and fold back double.

For 6 strips: Hold the webbing so that the back of the hook faces you. Insert finishing washer and 3/4" screw.

For 2 strips: Hold the webbing so that the front of the hook faces you. Insert the washer and screw.

Preliminary Placement of the Harness and Knee Support

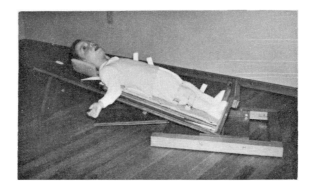

Put the standing board in a reclining position, held in place by the upper support board. Lay the child on the body board, his feet touching the footboard, his head on the headrest.

Harness. Center the harness on the child's body, the sides fitting snugly.
Mark on the body board with a pencil –
Right side: where the harness and webbing touch the surface.
Left side: where the harness touches the surface. Fold under the excess, as this is where you added the 3" extra length, leaving 3/4" to insert the washers and 3/4" screws. Refer to sketch 1 on page 12. Mark, at the shoulder level, where the shoulder straps touch the standing board.

Knee Support. Place the canvas between the child's knees, center and mark the two center holes. Tuck the canvas snugly around knees and mark where the sides and webbing touch the surface.

Remove the child from the standing board.

Attaching the Harness and Knee Support

Use 3/4″ finishing washers and screws to fasten the harness and webbing.

Harness

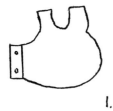

I.

Left side. Place the harness on the marked body board. Fold under excess, as explained on previous page and insert two washers and screws (1). Screw into position.

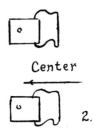

Center

2.

Right side. Place two hooks, with the back facing you, at the marks on the board. The doubled ends of the 3 1/2″ webbing extend toward the center (2). This enables the harness to encircle the child's body. Screw into place.

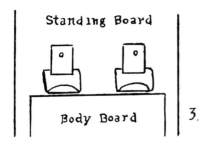

Standing Board

Body Board

3.

Shoulder level. Place two hooks, with the front facing you, where the shoulder straps touch the standing board. Screw webbing into place on the standing board so that the hook is on the shoulder marking and the webbing extends upward (3).

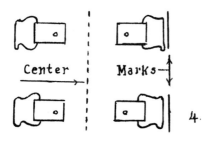

Center   Marks

4.

Knee Support. Place the canvas support on the marked body board and screw through the metal plate with two 3/4″ screws. Take the remaining four hooks, with the back facing you, and place them on the marked body board with the webbing facing toward the center (4). Screw into position.

Slide Buckle Placement.

Place the slide buckles on the straps of the harness and knee support.

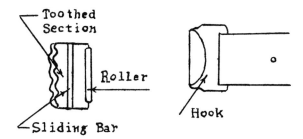

Hold the slide buckle so that the roller faces the hook.

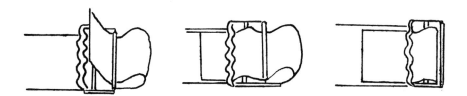

Thread webbing up, over the slide bar and down into the toothed section.

When the buckle is hooked and the strap tightened, the buckle will lock into place. If it fails to lock, rethread your webbing.

USING THE STANDING BOARD

Put the standing board in the reclining position and place the child on the body board, as shown in the picture on page 11. Fasten the harness, sides and top, and the knee support. Raise the board to the upright position and secure the lower support board with the catch strip and wedge lock on the back of the standing board. Place the table, page 16, in front of the child. For additional support use the padded metal pieces which are described on pages 18 and 19.

Place the feet in good alignment. If the feet move, strips of wood can be screwed to the footboard to provide channels. If one leg is shorter than the other, insert a piece of wood the proper thickness, under the shorter leg.

The child's tolerance for standing should be built up gradually. Start with ten minutes twice a day and build up to forty minutes or longer.

To Correct a Poor Position of the Knee

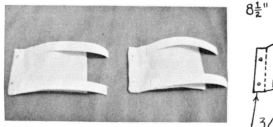 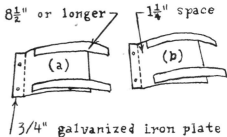

If the child's knee is in poor alignment after a reasonable trial period, unscrew the knee support and remove the metal piece. Cut the canvas in half and sew up the open ends. Screw into place putting the screwed section on the side where the knee bends out of position (a). Re-position the hooks. The other half of canvas (b) can be screwed into the same position as before the removal of the metal plate. Use finishing washers with four 3/4" screws. If you cut new pieces of canvas, sew in a 3/4" piece of 22 gauge iron on the side where the screws are inserted.

To Correct a Poor Trunk Position

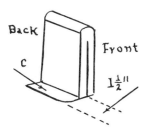

If the child has poor trunk alignment use the same type of metal support that you use for the table support, page 18. The support should be high enough to clear the harness when the child is in the standing board. Pad the metal, going to the bottom on the back as well as the front. Glue the leather piece on the top side of the metal (c).

Attaching on Standing Board. Screw the supports into place — one under the arm and the other at the hip. This will usually be sufficient to give the desired result.

TABLE

MATERIALS

3/4″ ply
Pine 1 3/4″ x 1 3/4″
3/4″ quarter round
1 1/4″ flathead #6 screws
Eight 3″ carriage bolts 1/4″ diam.
Eight 1/4″ washers
1/4″ drill
Screw-Guide
Crack filler
Wilhold glue
Polyurethane liquid plastic
100C garnet paper
Shellac

MEASUREMENT OF CHILD

1. Distance from bent elbow to floor
2. Length of arm
3. Newspaper pattern cut-out of child's waist

CONSTRUCTION

Use 3/4″ ply unless otherwise indicated. Use the Screw-Guide #1465 for #6 screws for all holes.

Top   Cut 1

Width: newspaper pattern of child's waist plus length of arm

Length: length of arm x 2

Length: if used with standing board, page 5 — width of frame plus 9″

Cut-out: use newspaper pattern of child's waist

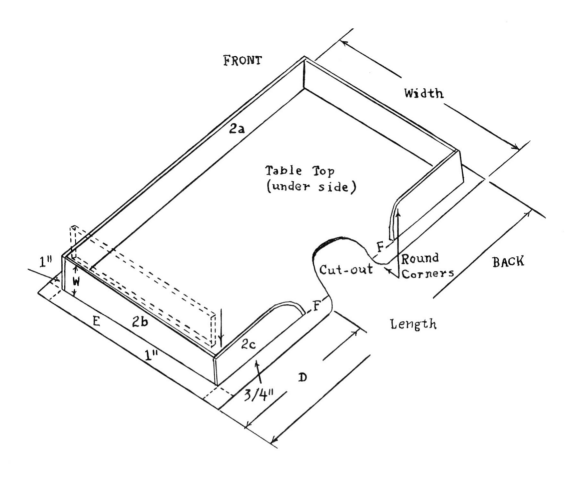

Apron

Width: 2 1/2 " or any measurement over 2 "
Length: Front piece (2a)
   Cut 1 the length of the table minus 2"

Side pieces (2b)
Cut 2 the width of the table minus 3 1/4"

Back piece (2c) Cut 2. Measure the distance from the edge of the table to the cut-out (D). Subtract 1 " (E) and 2 " to 3 1/2" (F). This measurement depends on the size of your table. The cut-out can be made larger as the child grows. Leave enough space so that the back piece will not be in the way when you cut the hole larger. Round corner on both back pieces.

Legs

Cut 4 using 1 3/4 " x 1 3/4 " pine.

Height: distance from bent elbow to floor

If table is to be used with the standing board, page 4

Add 1 1/2 " (platform plus footboard) to height.

If table is to be used with a standing box, page 24

Add 1/2 " or 3/4 " — the thickness of the platform on which the child is standing.

Assembly

Glue apron on the underside of the top. The side pieces (2b) going inside of the front piece (2a) and two back pieces (2c). See diagram on the preceeding page. Screw in from the top of the table using 1 1/4" screws. Countersink the heads.

Mount each leg in the corner of the apron, drilling a 1/4 " hole through the side, front piece, and leg. Stagger the two holes. Insert a 3 " carriage bolt into each hole, add a 1/4 " washer, and tighten the nuts.

Ledge

A ledge can be placed on the front and two sides of the table to prevent toys from rolling off. Cut 3/4" quarter round to fit and screw into place using 1 1/4" screws. Screw up into the molding from the underside of the table top.

Finish

Sand the table and the legs. Fill the screw holes in the table top with crack filler which you might want to stain to match the wood color. Use several coats of polyurethane liquid plastic to protect the wood.

Table Supports   (Can be used on one or both sides)

Materials

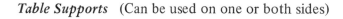

Galvanized iron — gauge 16	#6 3/4" screws and finishing washers
1/8" metal drill	
Leather scrap	Plastic material or denim
Tin snips	Rug scrap or foam rubber

Procedure.

Cut the metal 4 3/4″x 4″. This will make the support slightly over 3″ high when the padding is on which is usually satisfactory as the support should not be so high as to touch the child's armpit. Round all the corners. Drill two holes close to the bottom of the metal. Score 1″ up from the bottom and bend. Cover both sides of the metal with rug padding or foam rubber, overlapping 1/4″ on three sides.

Bring the padding all the way down on the front side and to within 3/4″ of the bottom on the back. Sew together with plastic material or denim, tuck in, and sew open sides together with string.

Attaching the Metal Support.

Cut a piece of leather (a) corresponding to the shape of the bottom of the metal piece. Punch through the pre-drilled holes in the metal to score holes in the leather. Use a leather punch or anything sharp.

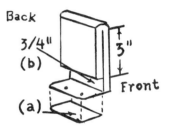

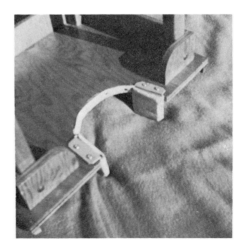

1.   2.

Saw out from the cut-out in the table a segment from one or both sides (1) that will permit the padded support to fit into place without making the opening too small. Turn the table upside down. Place the support into the sawed out section, placing the (b) section against the table. Place the leather (a) on top of the metal, lining up the pre-scored holes. Screw into place using 3/4″ screws and finishing washers (2).

STANDING TABLE

For the child that has good head and trunk control.

MATERIALS

Two 4″ light tee hinges
One 3″ barrel bolt
Four 2″, 1/4″ diam. flat head stove bolts
Four 1/4″ washers
5/8″, 3/4″ 1 1/4″ #6 flat head screws
1/4″ drill
One 2 1/2″ safety hasp
One 1/2″ x 2 1/2″ swivel snap hook
One small screw eye

6″ light weight chain
3/4″ ply
Pine, 1 3/4″ x 1 3/4″
100C garnet paper
#1465 Screw-Guide for #6 screws
Brace and bit
Countersink
Four 1 1/4″ round head bolts 1/4″ diam.
Four 1/4″ washers
Polyurethane liquid plastic

MEASUREMENT OF CHILD

1. 3 1/2″ above waist to 3″ below buttocks
2. 2″ above knee to 2″ below knee
3. Length of shoe

CONSTRUCTION

Use 3/4 " ply unless otherwise indicated. Use the Screw-Guide for all holes. The seemingly senseless directions in measuring for the door and door supports will enable you to have a perfect fit no matter what size table top you decide on. Sand the pieces as you go and put on several coats of liquid plastic for a protective coating.

Table

Build the table proceeding as described on pages 16 through 18. Add 2 " to the depth of cut-out on the table top to allow for the snug fit that will result from adding a door.

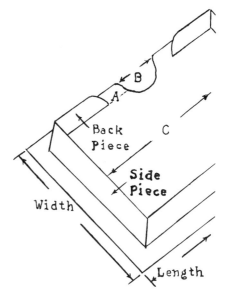

Door

    Width: distance from cut-out to back
        piece (A)
        Subtract 1″
        Double this figure
        Add width of cut-out (B)

    Length: 3 1/2″ above waist to 3″
        below buttocks

Round the upper corners.

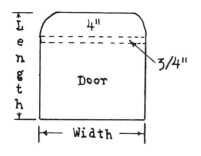

Measure 4 " down from the top edge and mark lightly. This part of your door will project above the table surface. Add 3/4" for the thickness of the table and mark lightly.

21

Door Supports   (Two L-shaped pieces)

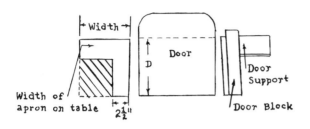

Cut 2 reversing the pattern

Width: Subtract the door measurement from the table measurement and divide the figure by 2.

Door measurement: Width of door minus 1 ˝.

Table measurement: measure length of table from side pieces, indicated by (C) on sketch of table on the preceeding page. Subtract 5 1/2˝.

Length: Distance from the 4 3/4˝ mark to the bottom of the door (D) on the door support diagram above.

Door Blocks   Cut 2

Width: 2˝

Length: length of door support plus 3/4˝

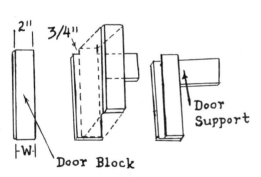

Assembly. Screw the door block on the door support leaving 1/2˝ on the inside edge and extending 3/4˝ at the top. Screw in from the back using 1 1/4˝ screws. Bolt the door support to the back pieces of the table 2 3/4˝ from the end. Use four 2˝ flat head stove bolts, the nuts and washers going on the inside. Countersink the heads of the bolts.

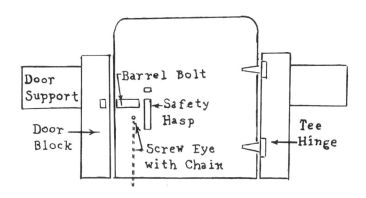

Door Support

Door Block

Barrel Bolt

←Safety Hasp

←Screw Eye with Chain

Tee Hinge

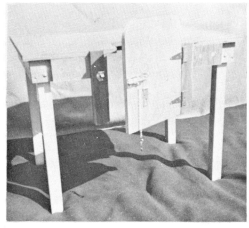

Screw the tee hinges on the door using 3/4″ screws. Screw the 3″ barrel bolt on the door using 5/8″ screws. The safety hasp is screwed, 5/8″ screws, at the end of the barrel bolt in a vertical position, the movable part at the bottom. Put your snap hook on the chain and attach it to the screw eye which is inserted below the barrel bolt. Mount the door on the door supports and screw the hinges into place on the right door block. Screw the barrel bolt catch on the left door block. When the barrel bolt is closed, the safety hasp can also be closed and secured by snapping the hook through the loop. This prevents young children from releasing the bolt when the child is standing in the table. The table can now be used for a child wearing long leg braces.

If you feel that the child might tip the table backwards, cut two pieces of 3/4″ ply, 1 3/4″ wide and extending 13″ beyond the back of the table. Screw to the legs using 1 1/4″ screws. This will stabilize the table.

Box For Standing Table

For the child not wearing long leg braces it is necessary to build a box for him to stand in.

Materials

3/4″, 1″, 1 1/4″ #6 flat head screws
Rug scraps
Eight 1 1/4″ 1/4″ diam. round head stove bolts
1/4″ washers
Wood, 1/4″, 1/2″, 3/4″ ply
Plastic material
Four 3″ angle irons
Sixteen #10 3/4″ screws

Sides   Use 1/4″ ply   Cut 2
Width: Add 3″ to shoe measurement
Length: the same as the table leg minus the thickness of the platform the child will be standing on.

You can make the sides as long as you wish providing you build up the platform so that the table is the right height (see the third picture on the next page). As the child grows the built-up section can be lowered until you reach the platform.

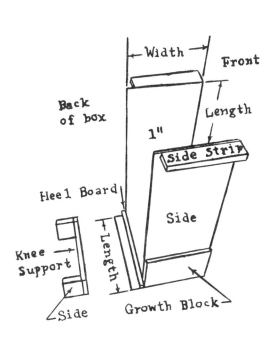

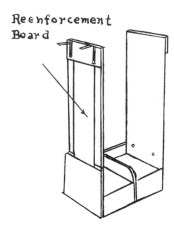

Side Strip Use 3/4″ ply Cut 2
  Width: 1 1/2″ to 2″. 3 1/4″
    if using the angle irons
  Length: same as width of
    side minus 1″.

Growth Blocks Use 3/4″ ply
Cut 2
  Width: same as side measure-
    ment
  Height: 4″ to 9″

Platform Use 1/2″ or 3/4″ ply
Cut 1
  Width: add 1 1/4″ to width
    of side
  Length: measure the distance
    between the door sup-
    ports. Add 1 1/2″ for the
    thickness of the two
    growth blocks. Add 1/2″
    for the two 1/4″ sides.

Heel Board Use 3/4″ ply Cut 1
  Width: 1 1/4″ or as wide as
    necessary
  Length: as long as the plat-
    form

Knee Support Use 3/4″ ply
  Front Cut 1
  Width: 2″ above to 2″ below
    the knee of child
  Length: the distance between
    the door supports
  Sides Cut 2
  Width: 2 1/2″
  Length: the width of the
    front of the knee support

Reenforcement Board Use 1/2″
ply Cut 2 (optional)
  Width: 5″
  Length: from growth block
    to side strip

Assembly

Screw side strips to the outer top edge of each side, the front edges flush using 3/4″ screws. If using the wider 3 1/4″ piece of wood, screw flat to side. Screw two 3″ angle irons to each piece using 3/4″ screws.

Screw, from beneath, the growth blocks to the platform the front edges flush. Use 1 1/4″ screws or 1″ if 1/2″ ply is used. Bolt the sides to the growth blocks using 1 1/4″ bolts, with the heads going on the inside. Tighten the nuts after inserting the washers. If using the reenforcement boards, center them above the growth blocks and screw them into place using 3/4″ screws.

Screw, from beneath, the heel board to the back of the platform, touching the back edges of the side. Use 1 1/4″ screws or 1″ if 1/2″ ply is used.

Screw the sides on to the knee support using 1 1/4″ screws. Pad the front and cover with textured plastic material.

Screwing the Box to the Underside of the Table

Remove the door and turn the table upside down. Place the box in position so that the back of the box lines up with the back of the table, the sides touching the door support. Screw the side strips or the angle irons to the table top using four 1 1/4″ screws or 3/4″ #10 screws for the angle irons. Turn the table right side up and replace the door.

Standing The Child

Place the child in the table with his heels against the heel board. Close the door. Place the padded knee support against his knees and gently push the child into an upright position. Mark the location of the sides of the knee support. Remove the child before bolting the sides of the knee support to the sides of the box. Use four 1 1/4″ round head bolts putting the heads on the inside. Tighten the nuts after inserting 1/4″ washers.

A 13″ extension may be added if you feel that the child may tip the table backwards.

The child's legs may be separated by a board.

Strips of wood will keep the feet in good alignment. Shoe cut-outs are another way. Remove the heel board when using the cut-out. Use 3/4 " ply for either process.

As the child grows the table can be raised by bolting on new legs and raising the box inside the growth blocks. The cut-out can be enlarged as well.

CHAIR FOR USE ON A HIGHCHAIR

This chair is for use on a highchair from which is removed the back, arms, and footrest.

MATERIALS

#6 screws — 1/2″, 5/8″, 3/4″, 1″
Polyurethane liquid plastic
Four 1 1/2″ angle irons
1/2″ wood bit
Two 1″ angle irons
Tacks — 1/4″, 3/4″
Electric jig saw
Screw-Guide
Ply — 1/4″, 1/2″, 3/4″
100C garnet paper
Rug padding
Plastic material

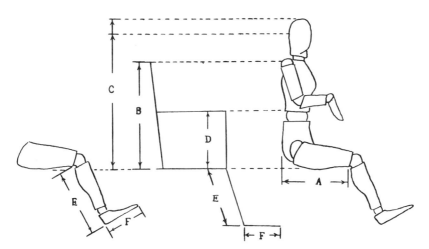

MEASUREMENT OF CHILD IN SITTING POSITION

A. Depth: buttock to bend of knee
B. Back of chair: buttock to shoulder
C. Headrest: buttock to middle of head; buttock to top of head
D. Height of side: buttock to bent elbow
E. Leg rest: bend of knee to heel
F. Footboard: length of foot

Width: width of child at hips
Tray cut-out: newspaper pattern of child's waist
Canvas harness: make newspaper pattern, page 9.
Cutting and sewing directions, page 42

CONSTRUCTION

Use the Screw-Guide #1465 for #6 screws for all holes. Sand and use liquid plastic as you go, particularly before tacking on the padding.

Seat
Use 1/2" ply   Cut 1
Width: 12"
Length: depth of child.
   Add 4"

Back
Use 1/2" ply   Cut 1
Width: same as seat
Length: buttock to
   shoulder. Add 1/2"

Sides
Use 1/2" ply   Cut 2
Width: 9" or wider
Length: depth of seat

Tray Ledge
Use 3/4" ply   Cut 2
Width: 1 1/4"
Length: the length of the side

Sides and Seat Wedges

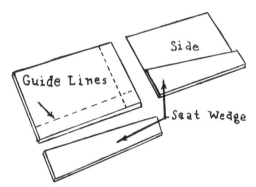

How to Measure for the Seat Wedge

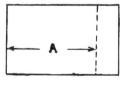

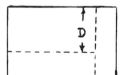

1. On one side mark, from the front, the depth of the child (A). Refer to the diagram of the manikin on page 29. Add 2" for padding, thickness of back, and "dead" space behind the child's buttocks.

2. From the top, mark the height of the side (D). Add 1" for padding and thickness of seat.

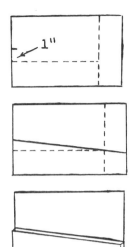

3. Mark, from the front, 1″ up from the dotted line. Increase this measurement if you wish more of an inclined seat.

4. Draw a line from this mark through the bisected line.

5. You now have a wedge shape which you measure and duplicate on 3/4″ ply. Cut two, reversing the pattern.

Assembly

Screw the seat wedges to each side using 1″ screws. Screw the tray ledge to the upper outer edge of each side using 1″ screws. Place the seat on the wedges and fasten into place using 1 1/2″ angle irons and 1/2″ screws into seat section. Use 5/8″ screws into seat wedge section.

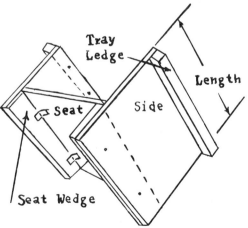

Mark 3 " down from the top, 3 1/2 " up from the bottom as well as the center. Working from the center line, mark out the width measurement of the child. Add 1/2 " on each side for the channel. Bore a hole in the top and bottom of the channel with a 1/2 " bit and complete the job with the electric jig saw. Sand the edges smooth.

Make a light guideline on the seat which indicates the depth of the child (buttock to bend of knee) plus 2" which allows for padding and thickness of the back. Place the back on the seat, in front of the guide line. The bottom edge flush with the surface of the seat or at an angle that you feel would be suitable.

1. Mark, on the side, the wedge shape made by the back meeting the seat. Measure and duplicate on 3/4 " ply. Cut two, reversing the pattern. Screw the side to the wedges using 1 " screws.

2. Go in from the front and screw the back to the wedges using 3/4 " screws.

3. For more stability screw two 1 " angle irons on the back.

4. If the child is hyperactive, the back may be made more secure by screwing a 1/4" piece of plywood to each side using 1/2 " screws.

Headrest Support

Support Stick

Use 3/4″ ply   Cut 1
Width: 1 3/4″
Length: buttock to top of head.
    Add 1″

Headrest
  Materials

Galvanized iron 16 to 22 gauge
1/2 yard plastic or 1 yard denim
Rug scraps
3/16″ metal drill
Two 3/16″ round head bolts, washers
Tin snips

Procedure

Support Stick. Bolt on the back of the chair using two 1 1/2″, 1/4″ diameter flat head bolts. Countersink the heads of the bolts which are on the front side.

Headrest. If the child has minimal head control the V-shaped headrest is used, page 7. Use 22 gauge galvanized iron. A galvanized iron piece, 16 gauge, can be cut 6″ x 11 1/4″ rather than 4 1/2″ x 11 1/4″ if a larger head rest is desired. This can be set lower on the support stick so that the child cannot drop his head under the padded sides. When making the larger headrest use foam rubber padding and cover with denim. Make a removable cover as well which can be washed. Place the headrest on the support stick 1″ down from the top. Make holes in the wood by drilling through the holes in the metal. Bolt into place with two 3/16″ bolts. Insert a washer before tightening the nut.

Foam Rubber Head Support

Materials

2" foam rubber
Hack saw blade
Four 1 1/2" bolts 1/4" diam. flat head
#6 finishing washers

For more support cut a circle into a 1/2" ply board (headboard) using as the diameter the width of the child's head. Leave 1 1/4" clearance on top and bottom. The board can be any size.

Cut a piece of foam rubber with a hack saw blade about the same size as the headboard. Cut a hole in the foam rubber to duplicate the hole in the headboard. Cover the foam rubber with denim and make a removable cover as well. You will need two support sticks which can be bolted in place with 1 1/2" bolts or screwed with 1" screws. Screw the headboard on the support sticks and the foam rubber support to the headboard using four 1/2" screws and finishing washers.

Headboard Support

For the child who needs only minimal head support, a padded 1/2" ply board can be screwed to the support stick using 1" screws. If the board is only there to prevent the child from throwing his head back, blocks of wood, 1" or 1 1/4", will set the board further back.

Padding the Back and Seat

Cut the padding from rug scraps, rug padding or whatever is available. Cut the plastic material larger than the padding and fold over. It can be sewn with string for easier handling. Tack into place using 3/4 " tacks.

False Sides

Since the seat of the chair is wider than the measurement of the child, make it the proper width by inserting false sides. Take two pieces of 1/4" ply and cut to fit the side, as you did when you made the back more secure for the hyperactive child, page 32. Put enough layers of padding to build out each side so that the width of the chair corresponds to the width of the child. Place the padding and plywood on your plastic material, as shown on the left of the picture above. Pull edges of the plastic tightly over the wood and tack into place using 1/4 " tacks. Screw into position in your chair using four 5/8 " screws.

Tray

The tray, when in position on the tray ledges, is held in proper alignment by the guide boards. The child cannot push the tray upward or forward as it is held in place by the holding boards underneath and two sections of hinged wood, the tray lock, in the back.

Materials

1/4", 1/2 ', 3/4" ply
1/2", 3/4", 1" #6 screws
Two 2" steel narrow butt hinges *or*
Two 1 1/2" butt hinges
1/2" #4 screws

Polyurethane liquid plastic
Heavy cardboard
Wilhold glue
Crack filler

Tray   Use 1/2″ ply   Cut 1
> Width: width of chair from tray ledges.
>> Add 5″
> Length: from padded back of chair to front.
>> Add 5 1/2″

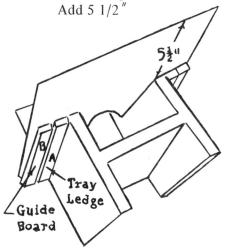

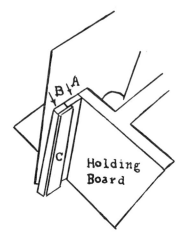

Guide Board (B)
> Use 3/4″ ply   Cut 2
> Width: 1 1/2″
> Length: long as tray ledge

Holding Board (C)
> Use 1/4″ ply   Cut 2
> Width: 2 3/8″
> Length: long as tray ledge

Cut-out: Use newspaper pattern of child's waist

Procedure

Center tray on chair and mark on under side where ledges are. Screw guide board (B) on under side of tray, screwing in from top of tray using four 1″ screws. Countersink all screw heads. Leave 1/16″ clearance from the tray ledge as the tray should not bind as it slides on and off. Glue one or two strips of poster board or heavy cardboard to each guide board before screwing on the holding board (C). The tray will now be loose enough to slide back and forth on the tray ledges like a drawer.

Finish

Fill the screw holes on the surface of the tray with crack filler which may be stained to match the wood. After it is dry, sand and give three or four coats of polyurethane liquid plastic.

Tray Lock

Slide the tray to the back of the chair.

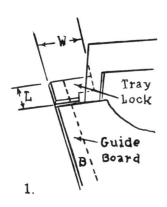

1.

Tray Lock   (Diagram 1)
Use 1/2″ ply   Cut 2
Width: from the outer edge of the guide board (B) to the back. Add 1/2″ so there will be an overlap on the back of the chair.
Length: as long as the extending guide board.

Notching the Tray Lock
(Diagram 2)
Width: 1/2″
Length: (A) Measure from the tray to the back of the back section. Add 1/4″. This part of your tray lock will be movable and the 1/4″ will permit clearance of the back, which is at a slant.

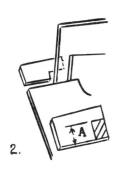

2.

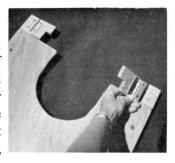

Cutting the Tray Lock into Two Sections
(Diagram 3)

Mark on the outer edge of the plywood the width of the guide board (B). Cut the wood on this line and the two sections will become D and E. Screw the D part of your lock to the guide board (B) using 3/4″ screws, placing it about 1/16″ from the tray. This will prevent the movable E section from binding. Hinge the two sections together using a 2″ butt hinge and 1/2″ screws.

The tray can now be put on the chair and the locks, flipped into a flat position, will prevent the child from pushing the tray forward. To remove the tray, flip the tray locks to an upright position.

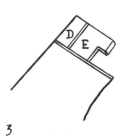

3

Tray Supports

May be used if the child has a tendency to lean to one side. Use on one or both sides.

Follow the directions for making the table supports, page 18, using 1/2" screws if your tray is constructed of 1/2 " ply.

A ledge of .3/4 " round which has had several coats of liquid plastic may be screwed on to the tray. Screw up from the bottom using 3/4 " screws.

If a ledge is not screwed on to the tray, round the edges as shown in the pictures above.

Attaching Chair on Highchair

Materials

    Four 1″ angle irons
    Four 1 1/4″ 3/16″ diam. round head stove bolts and washers
    3/16″ drill
    3/4″ #6 screws

Procedure

Screw angle irons to the side of the chair. Position on the highchair and bolt into place. If the chair unit is too large for the angle irons to fit on the top of the highchair, screw the angle irons on the inner side of the seat wedges. Mark where the holes are on the angle irons so that corresponding holes may be drilled through the seat of the highchair. Anchor into place with 3/16″ bolts. Slip washers on the bolts before tightening the nuts.

Footrest

Materials

1″, 1 1/4″ #6 screws
Two 2 1/2″, two 3″ 1/4″ diam. round head stove bolts
1/2″, 3/4″ ply
1/4″ drill

Footboard (See diagram on opposite page)

Use 1/2″ ply   Cut 1
> Width: measure from the seat the distance from the bend of the child's knee to the heel (E). Measure the spread of the high-chair legs at this point and add 2 1/2″ (1 1/4″ overlap on each side)
> Length: length of child's foot plus 2 1/2″

Wedges

Use 3/4″ ply   Cut on the diagonal making two pieces
> Width: 4″
> Length: 2″ less than the length of the footboard

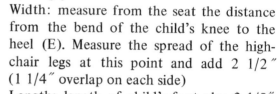

Assembly

Screw the back board on the underside of the footboard. Set in 1″. This will permit your footboard to be level when it is mounted on the highchair legs, as it will compensate for the slant of the legs. Screw in from the top both the back board and the wedges using 1″ screws. The wedges are set in 3″ from the end. Set them in further if necessary, as they must clear the legs of the chair. Screw through the back board into the wedges using four 1 1/4″ screws. Countersink all screw heads.

Mounting the Footrest on the Highchair Legs

Place the footrest down from the seat the distance from the bend of the knee to the heel (E). Drill two 1/4″ holes through the back board in the 3″ space left when you screwed the wedges in place. Drill through the legs as well. Insert the 3″ bolts into the top hole and the 2 1/2″ bolt into the bottom hole. Insert washers, thread on the nuts and tighten. Repeat on the other side.

Finish

Fill the screw holes on the surface of the footboard with stained crack filler. After it is dry, sand the surface, as well as the back board and the wedges. Give several coats of liquid plastic.

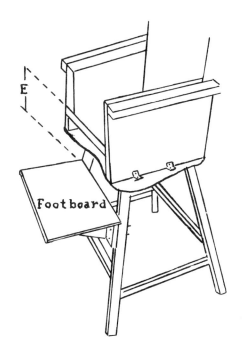

Harness

Materials

Light weight canvas
1 1/2 yd. corset webbing
Two #6 finishing washers and 1/2″ screws
Four 1″ corset hooks
Four 1″ slide buckles

Cut 2 strips 10″ long (side straps)

2 strips 6″ long (shoulder straps)
4 strips 4 1/4″ long

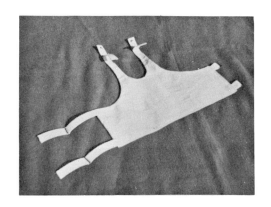

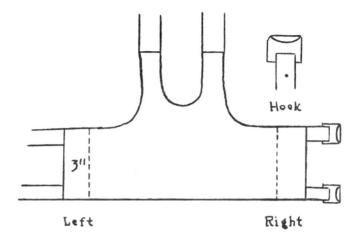

Hook

Left   Right

Procedure

Cut out the harness using a newspaper pattern of the child, page 9. Allow 3 extra inches on each side for going through the channels on your chair and strapping it in the back. Add 3″ to the bottom which is turned under. This can be let out as the harness shrinks from repeated washings.

Sew the harness leaving both sides and the tops of the shoulder open. Turn right side out and press flat. Insert the side straps in the left side about 1″ and sew. Center a hook on each 4 1/4″ strip so that the hook faces you. Refer to the diagram above. Fold back double and insert two strips in the right side of your harness about 1″ and sew. Be sure that the hooks are facing you otherwise they will be turned in when you go to buckle your harness. Sew in the shoulder straps. Place the slide buckles on the webbing. Refer to page 13 for directions on threading the webbing through the slide buckle. Take the remaining two folded 4 1/4″ strips and insert a 1/2″ screw and finishing washer. Line the straps up with the channels on the back of your chair or with the shoulder straps of your harness. Screw the straps into the back of the chair with the hooks facing you. If the hooks are level with the top of the chair, it is easier to attach the harness.

Placing the Child in the Chair

Seat the child in the chair. While holding him with the left hand, buckle the harness shoulder straps into the hooks on the back of the chair. Thread the side straps and hooks through the channels and hook in the back. Pull the side straps to the desired tightness.

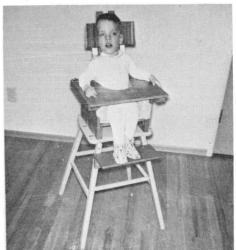

Tray

Slide on the tray and flip the tray locks down so that the tray is locked into position.

Growth Changes

The chair can be made larger as the child grows.

Making the Chair Deeper (Increasing the length of the seat)

Unscrew the side screws that are holding the back wedges (p. 32) and slide backwards until the seat is the desired depth. Rescrew the wedges which must now be trimmed to conform with the sides. Add on to the seat padding to conform with the new depth.

Making the Chair Wider

Unscrew the false sides, (p. 35) and remove some of the padding. On replacing, slide the sides back until they touch the back of the chair. You will find that because of the new depth, the false sides will not reach to the front of the chair. However, the child will continue to have the feeling of security because the chair is the proper width.

Making the Sides Higher

Remove the screws from the angle irons that are attached to the seat wedge (p. 31) as well as the screws that attach the seat wedge to the sides. Saw off 1″ or more from the bottom, then replace the sides and the seat. Make new false sides that will fit the new depth and height.

Lowering the Footrest

Remove the bolts from the back board (p. 40) and lower the footrest. New holes may have to be drilled as the space between the highchair legs gets wider as you drop down.

Tray

Enlarge the cut-out if necessary.

CHAIR TO BE SET ON THE FLOOR

This is a chair which is to be set on the floor and used with a table.

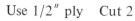

Side

Sides

Use 1/2″ ply   Cut 2
Width: same as seat measurement
Height: buttock to bent elbow plus bend of
    knee to heel

Support Boards

Use 3/4″ ply   Cut 2
Width: 2 1/2″
Length: width of seat minus 1 1/2″

Growth Blocks

Use 3/4″ ply   Cut 2
Width: 4″
Length: same as side

Support
Board — Growth
Block

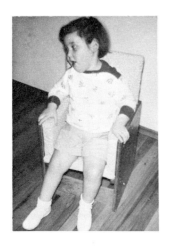 

Procedure

Construct the chair as described on pages 29 through 32 but omit the tray ledges. If the child has good head and trunk balance omit the channels for the harness. For added stability screw a support board in the front and back. Set the front one in 3″. The back support board may be flush with the back but raise it 1 1/4″ from the floor to provide toe space for the person handling the chair. Use four 1 1/2″ #6 screws to secure each board.

Growth blocks similar to those used on the standing table box, page 25, may be bolted on each side using four 2 1/2″ round head bolts, 1/4″ diameter. Be sure to put the bolt behind the front support board so that the child does not scratch his legs on the bolts that extend out on the inner side. Put a 1/4″ washer on each bolt before tightening the nut.

TABLE

Construct the table as described on pages 16 through 19. The back pieces, 2c (refer to the diagram on page 17) must be short enough to permit the table to clear the chair. For the leg height, add 1/2″ to the height of the side of your chair. The table will then be high enough to clear the chair.

CHAIR INSERT FOR A WHEELCHAIR

This is a chair unit that fits inside the wheelchair.

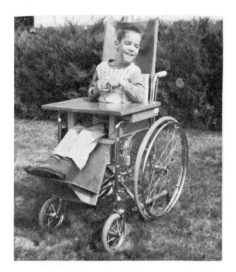 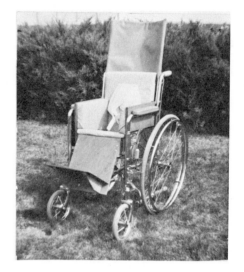

Get measurements of the child, page 29. The measurements of the wheelchair will give you the sides and seat of the chair insert.

Sides

    1/2″ ply   Cut 2
    Width: from the wheelchair seat to the top of the arm rest.
        Add 1/8″ if the arm rest is padded
    Length: the depth of the wheelchair

Seat

    1/2″ ply   Cut 1
    Width: the width of the wheelchair seat
        (The width of the wheelchair is the distance between the tubular framework.)
    Length: as long as the sides

Back

    1/2″ ply   Cut 1
    Width: width of seat
    Length: buttock to shoulder.
        Add 1/2″

Procedure

Construct the chair as described on pages 29 through 32. Omit the harness channels as the harness would be difficult to buckle because of the back of the wheelchair. Omit the tray ledges as the arm rests on the wheelchair serve the same purpose. However, if the child's measurements from the bent elbow to buttocks exceeds the measurement of the height of the wheelchair arms put the tray ledges on the sides of the chair insert as described on page 31.

Headrest

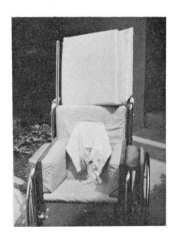
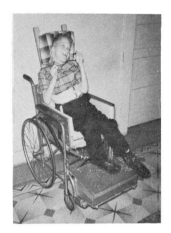
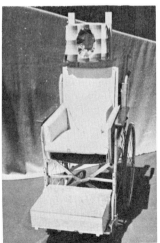

The type of headrest used, page 33, depends upon the needs of your child. If the wheelchair has the hook-on headrest attachment you do not need to build one on the chair, as a small pillow behind the child's head will accomplish the same result. For more permanence, cover a piece of foam rubber with naugahyde. Leave grooves on the outer edges so it can be slipped over the extending rods of the headrest attachment. The cushion pictured above, on the left, is 12 1/2″ wide, 14″ high and 2 1/2″ thick. The overall measurement is 16 3/4″ wide and 15″ high.

Footboard

The footboard can be built up to the proper height and mounted on the footrest of the wheelchair or it may be possible to raise the foot pedals.

If the child is small or if there are no foot pedals, a footboard can be built on to the chair unit.

Materials

1/2″, 3/4″ ply
1″, 1 1/4″ #6 screws
Four 1 1/2″ angle irons
Four 2 1/2″ diam. flat head bolts
Four 1/4″ washers 1/4″ diam.

Support Blocks

Use 3/4″ ply   Cut 2
Width: distance from padded seat to the
    bottom of the side
Length: 4 1/2″

Leg Rest

Use 1/2″ ply   Cut 1
Width: wide as seat of chair insert
Length: bend of knee to heel plus 4 1/2″
    growth space

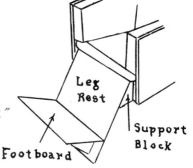

Footboard

Use 1/2″ ply   Cut 1
Width: same width as leg rest
Length: length of child's foot plus 1 1/2″ to 2″

Wedges

Use 3/4″ ply
Cut on the diagonal making 2 pieces
Width: 3″
Length: length of footboard minus 3/4″

Backboard

Use 3/4″ ply   Cut 1
Width: 3″
Length: width of footboard minus 3 1/2″

Procedure

Support Blocks. Using the 2 1/2″ bolts attach to the sides of the chair. Countersink the heads which are on the outer side. Use 1/4″ washers before tightening the nuts.

Footboard. Screw together. Refer to the procedure on page 40. Attach to the leg rest, measuring down from the top — the measurement being from the bend of the child's knee to the heel. Screw in from the back into the wedges and backboard with 1 1/4″ screws. For additional support use two 1 1/2″ angle irons underneath.

Leg Rest. Attach to the support blocks, screwing in from the top side with four 1″ screws. For additional support, use two 1 1/2″ angle irons underneath which can be screwed into the support blocks.

Wedges and Backboard. Refer to the procedure on page 40.

Canvas Binder

The child can be held securely by a canvas binder which can be bolted on to the back of the chair and threaded through the padding through the slits cut into the fabric, set as far apart as the width of the child or it may be bolted on to the back of the chair going through the plastic material and padding.

 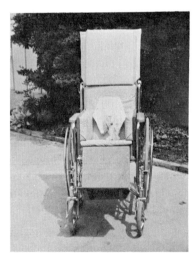

Materials

Light weight canvas
Three 1″ corset hooks and slide buckles (#7011)
3/16″ drill
Four 1″, Four 1 1/4″ 3/16″ diam. flat head bolts and washers
11 yds. corset webbing
Four #10 finishing washers

Width: measure the child from the waist to 2 " below the armpit
Length: measure around the child's waist. Add 6 "

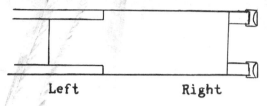

Left　　　　　　**Right**

Procedure

Cut canvas double thickness, stitch on three sides leaving one end open. Turn right side out and press. Cut 3 strips of webbing 8" long. Cut 3 strips 3 1/2" long. Center a hook on both 3 1/2" strips and insert them into the open end of the canvas, with the hook facing you. Sew the side. Sew the three 8" strips of webbing on the left side setting them in 5 ". Stitch 1 1/4" deep. If the canvas is under 5 " wide, two strips and two hooks will be sufficient.

Place the child in the chair unit and mark on the back where the binder will be attached — at the waist and 2" below the axilla. Remove ·the child and reverse your binder when you position it on the chair so that the hooks will be on the left side.

Pierce through the binder, plastic material and padding to the back of the chair, using a compass point or ice pick if you have one. Drill four 3/16" holes through the back. Use a knitting needle or anything round and smooth to make the holes in the canvas binder, plastic material, and padding large enough for the 3/16 " bolt. Put a #10 finishing washer on the bolt before inserting it into the holes. Put a washer on each bolt before tightening the nuts.

If more support is needed make a harness like the one used on the standing board (p. 9). Attach it the same way (p. 12) but bolt it on the left side using three 1 1/4 " 3/16 " diameter flat head bolts and #10 finishing washers. Buckle the right side and the shoulder straps.

Tray

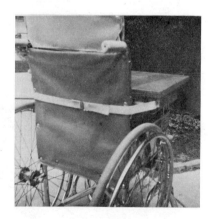

Tray locks can be made (refer to page 37), but an easy effective method of keeping the tray in place is to screw a piece of webbing on the outer side of the back end of each guide board. Sew a hook on the left section of webbing and put a slide buckle on the right side. Have each piece of webbing long enough so that you can buckle the ends together in the back of the wheelchair. Use two #6 3/4" screws and finishing washers.

To protect the wheelchair, take a strip of rug padding which has been covered with naugahyde or plastic material and tack it to the bottom of the chair unit as shown on the car seat, page 56.

CHAIR UNIT FOR SUPPORT OF THE CHILD WHO SLUMPS TO ONE SIDE

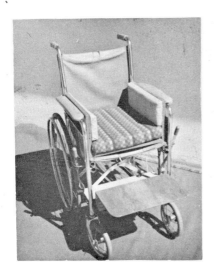

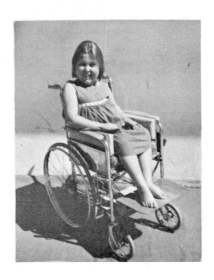

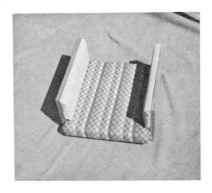

This unit is similar to the one described on the two following pages, however the sides are screwed directly to the seat using no seat wedges or back.

MATERIALS

1/4", 5/8", 3/4" ply
Plastic material
Denim
2", 3/4" foam rubber

Sides 5/8" or 3/4" ply
Seat 3/4" ply

Footrest

If there is no footrest, a footrest can be made for a folding wheelchair using the 1 1/4" size broom holders — gripper clips, which clamp on to the tubular chrome framework of the wheelchair. This enables the footrest to be removed when the wheelchair is folded.

CHAIR UNIT FOR SUPPORT OF THE CHILD WITH A BACK CURVATURE

This chair unit fits inside the wheelchair, and is made as described on page 46. Since the child may be sitting in the chair for long periods of time, thick foam rubber should be used for the cushion which is then covered with two denim covers — one to remain on permanently, the other which can be removed and washed. The false sides of the chair (p. 35) can be made so that they fit just above the cushion. This will hold the cushion in place but not tightly enough that it can't be slipped out.

MATERIALS

3/4 ″, 2″ foam rubber

Eight 1 1/4″ 3/16″ diam. round head bolts

Four 3 1/2″ angle irons

1/4 ″, 1/2″ , 5/8″, 3/4 ″ply

Eight 1 ″ 3/16 ″ diam. flat head bolts with washers

Denim

The supports which hold the child must be strong. This can be accomplished with the 3 1/2″ angle irons bolted, with 1 1/4″ bolts, into 3/4″ ply, heavily padded on both sides with foam rubber and covered with denim. Make two covers — one to remain on permanently and the other which can be removed. To measure the child for these supports, seat him in the chair unit and measure from the back of the chair to where it clears his rib cage in the front — the length. If you come to within an inch or two of his armpit you will have the right height. Allow for about 1 1/2″ of padding on three sides. The supports can be positioned where they will accomplish the optimum results. They are bolted into the back of the chair using the 1″ bolts and washers. Cover the angle irons and bolts with 3/4″ foam rubber which is covered with the plastic material.

Canvas Binder

The child may have a feeling that he is going to fall forward. If this is the case, put a canvas binder on. You will need two pieces of canvas long enough to go around the support and buckle in the front. The hook and buckle arrangement is the same as described on page 50. Attach each section right next to the support, using bolts if necessary and finishing washers, so the pressure of the tightened binder is exerted on the foam rubber and not directly on the child's rib cage. The attachment is made on the back of the chair.

CAR CHAIR

This chair unit works in the same way as a commercial car seat, being held in place by curved iron pieces. It is held in a level position by wedge-shaped pieces, bolted on to the back of the chair, which corresponds to the slant of the car seat.

If the chair is for a small child who will be unable to see out the window if the unit is on the car seat, notch the wedge as described on page 55. The weight of the chair unit as well as the child will then be distributed evenly along the slanted edge of the wedge. For the older child the chair unit may be placed directly on the seat.

MATERIALS

Four 1 1/2 " 1/4 " diam. flat head bolts
Four 1 1/4 " 3/16" diam. round head bolts
1" #6 screws
Four 1 1/2" angle irons
3/16 " metal drill
Wilhold glue
1/4" drill
2 pieces of iron — 26 " x 1 " x 1/8 " — have them curved, *or*
2 iron car seat supports from a discarded car seat

PROCEDURE

Construct the chair as described on pages 29 through 38, omitting the harness channels. For additional stability use four 1 1/2" angle irons in attaching the back to the sides. The headrest can be V-shaped or flat.

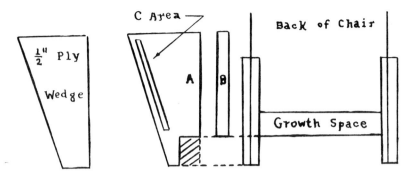

Cut two wedge shape pieces of 1/2″ ply. Notch it at the bottom to correspond to the 2″ growth space and the distance from the seat to the bottom of the side as shown on the diagram. Cut four support sticks (B) of 3/4″ ply 1 1/4″ wide. Glue and screw two of them into area (A) on both wedges using four 1″ screws. Bolt the wedges to the back of the chair using four 1 1/2″ flat head bolts, countersink the heads which will be on the inside

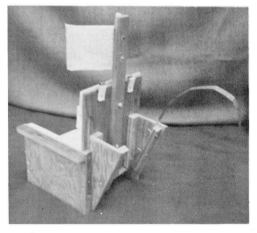

of the chair back. Glue and screw with four 1″ screws, the remaining two support sticks to the (C) area of your wedge setting it 1/4″ in from the edge. This will prevent the metal bolt heads from coming in contact with the car upholstery. Drill two holes through the wood and the iron car seat supports with the 3/16″ metal drill, at whatever height you wish the chair to rest. Bolt into place using two of the 3/16″ diamteter round head bolts.

Repeat on the other support stick. A strip of rug scrap glued on each wedge shape piece will make it easier on the car upholstery. The iron car supports might be covered with a sleeve of naugahyde or one made from the plastic material.

Securing the Child

The child can be held securely by a harness or a canvas binder. The harness, as described on page 9, will be attached in the same way as on the standing board, page 12. The canvas binder is described on page 49.

Tray

The tray (p. 36) will give additional security. The length of the tray need only be from the front to the back of the chair, leaving off the extra 5 1/2″ which might be cumbersome in the limited space of the car. Round the front edges of the tray.

This chair unit rests on the car seat.

Cut the wedges to correspond to the slant of the car seat, it need not be notched.

Round the front ends of each side and pad with a piece of rug scrap covered with plastic material. Glue a strip of rug scrap on each wedge where it touches the back of the car seat.

CAR TRAVEL – USING A CANVAS BINDER

A satisfactory way of traveling in the car with the child who has fairly good trunk and head balance is the use of a canvas binder. The binder is made (p. 49) and held in position on the back of the car seat by two strips of safety belt webbing which is installed. The seat belt buckled around the child gives him an added sense of security.

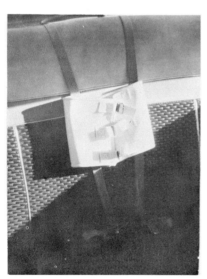

POTTY CHAIR

Get measurement of your child, page 29, including the width and length of the buttocks so that a hole of the proper size can be cut into the seat. Angle the saw when cutting the hole so that it will be beveled like the toilet seat. The hole can be notched at the end for a deflector.

Construct the chair as described on pages 29 through 38, however increase the height (width) of your sides as you did with the chair which is set on the floor, page 44. The support board is screwed in under the front part of the seat so there is room to slide the potty under the chair. The headrest may be omitted if the child has sufficient head balance. However, put one on if the child has a tendency to throw his head back.

The child will sit securely in the potty chair when the tray (p. 36) is locked into position. The harness can also be used (p. 41). If you pad and cover with plastic material, a piece of 1/4" ply the size of the seat, the chair can be used for play as well.

CHAIR ON WHEELS

This chair is used for the severely involved child who needs the security of a hole in the seat to sink down in to. The chair is on wheels for easier handling and is in two sections. It comes apart for easy loading into the car.

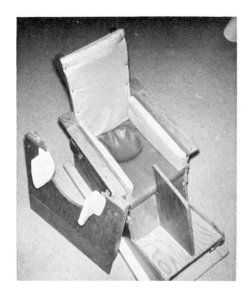

MATERIALS

In addition to those listed on page 29.

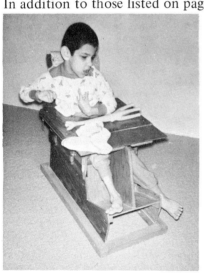

Heavy leather for seat
4 suitcase catches
Two 2" hard rubber swivel wheels
2 stationary wheels with screw plates
or 4 swivel wheels
Six 1 1/2" angle irons
1/4" drill
1 1/4" #6 screws
Four 3" 1/4" diam. carriage bolts
Four 1 1/2" 1/4" diam. flat head
stove bolts
1/4" washers for all bolts
Brace and 7/8" bit
7/8" dowel
Wilhold glue

TOP SECTION

Get measurements of the child, page 29. To get the depth of the seat turn the child over on his stomach and measure from the bend of the knee to the fold of the bottocks (A). Measure the width of the buttocks (B). Add 3 ˝ to A and B for the growth space.

Construction

Seat

Use 3/4 ˝ ply   Cut 1
Width: 14 ˝
Length: add 3 ˝ to A and B
Cut the hole in the seat using the (B) measurement as the diameter. The size of the hole should correspond to the width of the child at the hips. The hole should be set back from the front end of the board the distance from the bend of the knee to the fold of the buttock (A).

Construct the chair as described on pages 29 through 35, omitting the harness channels. When positioning the back allow 1/2″ distance from the hole to allow for padding.

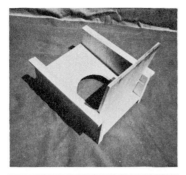

The wedges and angle irons secure the back to the sides, as described on page 32.

The type of headrest, if any, will vary depending on the needs of the child.

Pad the seat of the chair with rug padding, cutting out where the hole is. Cover with the leather. Wet the area that will fit down into the hole. Punch the leather to get a better contour and weight it down overnight or longer with a heavy sandbag or bowling ball.

Screw two wide strips of leather on the underside of the chair to reenforce the hole.

BOTTOM SECTION

Sides
Use 1/2″ ply   Cut 2
Width: 19″
Length: length of side of chair
   Add leg rest and footboard measurements
   Add 3/4″ for overlap

Support Board
Use 3/4″ ply   Cut 1
Width: 5″
Length: width of chair plus 1/8 ″

Support Stick
Use 3/4″ ply   Cut 2
Width: 2 ″
Length: length of side of chair

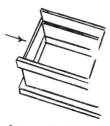

Support Board

Reenforcement Strips
Use 1/4 ″ ply
Width: 2 ″
Length: length of side of chair

Leg Rest
Use 1/2 ″ ply   Cut 1
Width: same as support board
Length: bend of knee to heel plus 3 ″

Support Sticks (b) for Leg Rest
Use 3/4 ″ ply   Cut 2
Width: 1 1/4 ″
Length: length of leg rest

Seat Wedge

b

a

Support Stick

Reenforcement Strip

Footboard
Use 1/2″ ply   Cut 1
Width: same as support board
Length: length of shoe plus 3 ″

Backboard
Use 3/4″ ply   Cut 1
Width: 2 ″
Length: width of footboard minus 1 1/2 ″

Footboard Wedge
Use 3/4 ″ ply   Cut on the diagonal
Width: 3 ″
Length: same length as the footboard

Procedure

Set the chair on the side piece 3/4″ in from the back and down 3 1/2″. Mark where the side of the chair touches the board and where the leg rest and footboard will be placed. Use your own judgment on the angle. Remove the chair.

Screw the support sticks (a) and (b) in from the sides using 1″ screws. Screw in the support board 1″ above the support stick (a) using four 1″ screws. It will fit into the 3/4″ space left in the back. A 1 1/2″ angle iron may be used on each side as well for added security. Use eight 5/8″ screws. On the bottom of each side, glue and screw in the reinforcement strips using 5/8″ screws. If necessary reenforce the sides with 2″ wide pieces of 3/4″ ply place upright beneath the support sticks (a).

Screw the leg rest to the support sticks (b) using four 3/4″ screws. Screw the wedges and backboard to the footboard using eight 1″ screws. The backboard goes flush with the back. The footboard assembly is on page 40. Place the chair into the bottom section and measure from the seat, the distance from the bend of the knee to the heel. Mark lightly and at this mark place your footboard. Screw the wedges in from the side using four 1″ screws.

Catch Boards

The catch boards, one screwed on the top section and the other on the bottom section, are the boards to which the suitcase catches are screwed.

 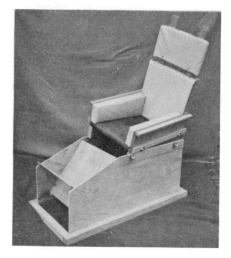

Catch Board — Top
Use 3/4" ply   Cut 2
Width: 1 1/2"
Length: length of chair side

Catch Board — Bottom
Use 1/4" ply   Cut 2
Width: 2 1/2"
Length: length of side on bottom section of chair

With the chair in the bottom section place the top catch board on the side and screw into place using three 1 1/4" screws. Place the bottom catch board under the top catch board and screw into place using three 3/4" screws. Repeat on the other side. Screw the two suit case catches on the top catch board and the spring lock part of the catch on the bottom catch board. Use 5/8" screws. When the catches are latched the chair will not come apart.

Frame

Use Pine 1 3/4" x 1 3/4"
Cut 2   Width: as wide as chair — end pieces
Cut 2   Length: as long as side pieces plus the two end pieces (3 1/2") (Refer to the pictures of the frame on the chairs above.)

Put frame together with the four 1 1/2" angle irons. Use 5/8" screws. Chisel out space where the angle irons will go as the frame fits snugly against the chair. Bolt the frame to the chair using four 3" carriage bolts. Use washers on bolts before tightening the nuts.

Hand Grip

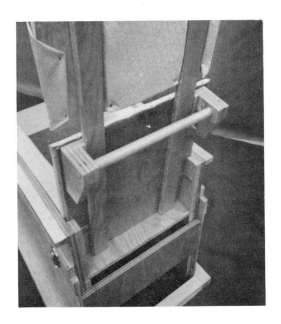

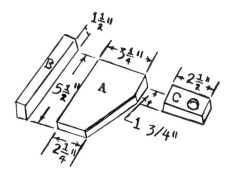

Cut section A, B, and C. Glue and screw section B to A using two 1 1/4" screws. Drill the 7/8" hole in section C about 1/2" from the outer edge. Glue and screw C to A using two 1 1/4" screws. Remove the padding from your chair back and drill two 1/4" holes through the B section and the back. Countersink the holes on the inside of the chair back and insert two 1 1/2" flat head bolts through the back and the B section. Put on washers before tightening the nuts. Repeat on the other side but leave the nuts loose. Measure the distance from the inner edge of one A section to the other — this will give you the length of your dowel. Insert the dowel and tighten nuts on the B section.

Cut the tray, pages 35 through 38. Use tray locks to secure the tray to the chair. If the child leans to either side, put on the tray supports. If the child feels insecure without the pressure of the tray against his body, pad the cut-out.

The chair may have a divider on the leg support, cut high enough to touch the tray. Screw it on to the leg rest, using 1 1/4″ screws, coming up from the under side. Cut a groove in the footboard as wide as the divider. The footboard can then be lowered as the child grows.

Growth Changes

The important measurement in this type of chair is the measurement from the bend of the knee to the fold of the buttocks (A on diagram, p. 60) and the size of the hole the child sits in. The easiest way to adjust the seat is to remove the screws from the angle irons which holds the seat to the seat wedge (p. 31) and slip the seat out. Cut a new seat, with the proper hole size and "A" measurement. Replace after giving it several coats of liquid plastic. For other changes like moving the back of the chair back, adjusting the false sides and footrest, follow the suggestions for growth changes found above and on page 43.

Modifications

Gusset

If you find that the leather covering the hole in the seat has not stretched sufficiently to give the child a sense of security, cut the leather with a razor blade following the outline of a plus (+). Fold back the pointed pieces and tack them to the underside of the seat. Make a gusset out of another piece of leather or suade about four inches deep and slightly larger than your hole. Screw it in place using 5/8" screws and #6 washers. Reenforce with leather strips.

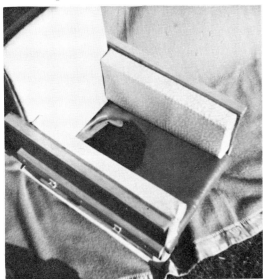

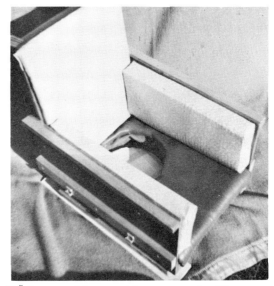

The hole can be filled in with a 1 1/2" foam rubber cushion covered with denim. Make two covers so that one can be removed and washed. The pillow gives the child a sense of contact with the bottom of the hole thereby giving him a greater sense of security.

CREEPER

This is a T-shape suspension creeper

MATERIALS

3/4″ ply
1 1/2″ x 1 1/2″ pine
1 1/4″ #6 screws
1/4″ drill
3/8″ drill
Three 2″ swivel ball bearing caster wheels
Three 3 1/4″ 1/4″ diam. round head stove bolts and washers

MEASUREMENT OF CHILD LYING DOWN

A. Distance between outstretched arms
B. Shoulders to buttock
L. Shoulders to pointed toe
H. Hip to knee
Newspaper pattern for harness (p. 9)

CONSTRUCTION

Use 3/4″ ply Cut 1
T-shape — Extensions 3″ wide
> Width: (A) distance between outstretched arms
> Add 5″

> Length: (L) shoulders to pointed toe
> Add 5″

The wider portion of the extension is the back board
> Width: 9″
> Length: (B) shoulders to buttocks plus 1″

Cut out the neck opening and round the corners
> Width: 4 1/2″
> Depth: 3/4″

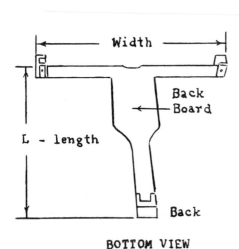

Width

Back Board

L - length

Back

BOTTOM VIEW

Apron (the wooden pieces that hold the legs)
Use 3/4″ ply
Cut 3 – 3″ x 3″   Cut 6 – 1 3/8″ x 3″
Glue and screw the apron to the extension. Screw from the top down using 1 1/4″ screws.

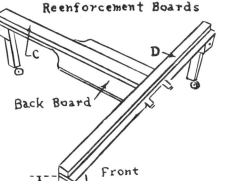

Reenforcement Boards

Back Board

Front

TOP VIEW

Reenforcement Boards
Use 3/4″ ply
Cut 1 (C) Width: 3″
    Length: the length of the creeper minus 3″
Cut 1 (D) Width: 2″
    Length: the width of the creeper
Screw the reenforcement boards into position on top of the frame. Countersink all screw heads.

Legs
Use 1 1/2″ x 1 1/2″ pine   Cut 3
Length: hip to knee
Set wheels into leg. Set legs into apron. Bolt through the side pieces putting on the washer before tightening the nut. Screw in from the front with a 1 1/4″ screw.

Pad and cover the backboard. Set the padding flush with the front end so that it covers the neck opening.

Canvas Harness

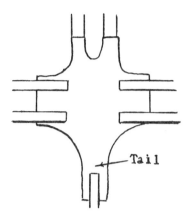

Materials

Canvas
7 slide buckles and hooks
1 3/4 yards of webbing
3/4 " screws and #6 finishing washers

Make newspaper pattern of child. The tail section goes between the child's legs like a diaper. The harness should not bind at the neck, the arms or the legs. The sides should touch the surface on which the child is lying.

Procedure

Cut and sew harness as described on page 9
Cut webbing: 2 strips 6" long (shoulder straps)
                5 strips 8" long (side and tail straps)
                7 strips 3 1/2" long
Center your hook on the 3 1/2" strips of webbing as described on page 11. On five of them, the back of the hook faces you and on two of them the front of the hook faces you. Insert the finishing washers and 3/4" screws.

Marking and Attaching The Harness

Place the child on the back board with his shoulders at the front of the frame. Place a pillow under his head for comfort. Proceed, as described on page 11, marking where the harness will be attached. Since there are side

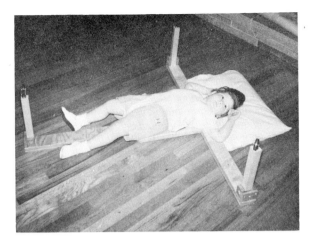

straps on both sides there will be no excess on the left side. Mark at the front of the frame where the shoulder straps touch. Remove the child. Take the five hooks with the back facing you and screw into place on the backboard. Screw the remaining two hooks, with the front facing you, on the front of the frame in the 1″ space in front of the (D) reenforcement board, see diagram on diagram on page 69.

Using the Creeper

Place child on back board. Fasten the harness — sides, tail, and top. Tighten the straps. Turn the frame over so that the child is suspended from the frame. If the child's knees do not touch the floor, loosen the straps. If the child is too heavy to turn over while strapped in the frame have the child kneel and position the frame over his body. Buckle the harness in place.

As the child grows, the creeper can be made higher by bolting on longer legs.

TUB FRAME

For the child who is heavy or hard to handle a tub frame is invaluable. It fits on the surface of the tub or can be elevated, so the mother doesn't strain herself lifting the child in and out of the deep recess of the bathtub.

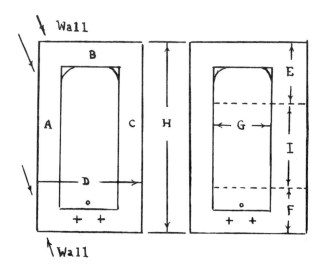

Measurement of Tub

A & B — the distance from tub to wall
C — the distance from the tub to the outer ledge, minus 1 3/4″
D — distance from the wall to outer edge of ledge, minus 1 3/4″
E — distance from the wall to the straight part of the tub
F — distance from the wall to 1 1/2″ in front of faucet
G — width of inner measurement of tub
H — overall length of tub.

ALUMINUM TUB FRAME

This frame is light and easy to handle.

Materials

Aluminum tubing 1 1/2″ diam.
1/8″, 3/8″ metal drills
Four 1/4″ self-locking nuts
Steel rod
3/4″ sheet metal screws — #8 with round Phillips head

Phillips screwdriver
Rubber belting
#8 finishing washers
High pressure spray hose 3/8″
10 yds. 2″ plastic webbing

 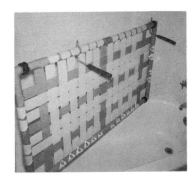

Use diagram of tub measurement as reference (on preceding page)
Width: distance from wall to outer edge of ledge, minus 1 3/4″ (D)
Length: overall length of tub (H) subtract (F)

Procedure

Cut the aluminum tubing, miter the corners and weld. Drill 1/8″ holes starting 6″ from the end of each side. Drill them 2 3/4″ apart and to within 6″ of the end. Drill two 3/8″ holes for the L-shaped frame holders, one 3 1/2″ from the front, the other about 3 1/2″ from the curve in the tub (3 1/2″ down from E in the diagram on the preceding page). Measure and cut the webbing, allowing about 3″ overlap on each side. Fold the end to make a point and insert a 3/4″ metal screw and washer. Screw one side and weave the webbing over one and under one when doing the other side. Put rubber belting on each of the four sides to protect the surface of the tub as shown in the pictures above.

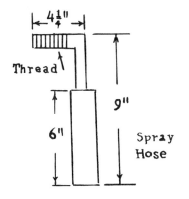

Frame Holder

Bend two pieces of 3/8″ steel rod to not quite a 90° angle. Thread the shorter end 3 1/4″ in. Put on a self-locking nut. Glue the hose on the opposite end for cushioning. Insert the two frame holders in the 3/8″ holes in the tub frame and put on the remaining two self-locking nuts.

Using The Frame

Place the tub frame on top of the tub, the inner side touching the wall, resting on the tub ledge (A). One end is resting on the tub ledge (B). The side that is resting on the outer tub ledge (C) is the side that has the two frame holders. Refer to the diagram on page 72.

Adjust the nuts so that the rubber hose is tight against the tub. Tighten the outer self-locking nut so that the frame is immovable.

Elevated Tub Frame

The frame may be elevated for the mother bathing an infant or young child. The aluminum framework fits the inner measurement of the tub and rests on the sides of the tub.

WOODEN TUB FRAME

Make the frame any length you wish; however, in making a frame the full size of the tub, allowing for the faucets, it may be too heavy to leave in one piece; therefore you would want to cut it into two sections as the frame illustrated.

Materials

3/4″ ply
3/4″, 1 1/4″ # 6 screws and finishing washers
Two 1 1/2″ angle irons

Polyurethane liquid plastic
Canvas or 2″ wide plastic webbing
Screw-guide

Use 1 1/4″ screws in constructing the frame. Use 3/4″ ply for all pieces. Glue all pieces.

Use diagram of tub measurement as reference (p. 72)

Side (A) Cut 1
   Width: distance from tub to wall (A) plus 3/4″
   Length: overall length of tub (H) subtract (F)

Side (C) Cut 1
   Width: distance from tub to outer edge minus 1″ (C)
   Length: overall length of tub (H) subtract (F)

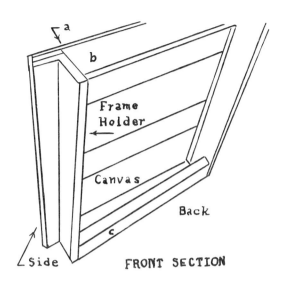

FRONT SECTION

Frame Holder Cut 2
> Width: 4″
> Length: (I) distance from
> (E) to (F)

End Pieces (a) Cut 2
> Width: 3″
> Length: width of inner
> measurement of tub
> plus width of sides A
> and C

End Pieces (b) and (c)
> Cut 2 or 4 if frame is cut
> into two sections
> Width: 3″
> Length: inner measurement
> of tub, subtract 1 1/2″

Procedure

Round the back lower corner of the frame holder and screw to the inside front edge of side A and side C. The frame holder is shorter than the side so it will clear the curve of the tub. Screw the end piece

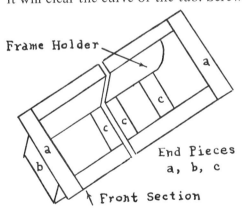

End Pieces a, b, c

Front Section

(a) into position on the front and back end
(b) between the two frame holders
(c) in a flat position at the rounded corner of the frame holder. Use two 1 1/2″ angle irons to hold more securely. Use 3/4″ screws.

Cut your frame into two sections and put an end piece (c) on each side of the sectioned frame. Give the frame several coats of liquid plastic. Screw strips of webbing into place on the frame as described on page 73 or use 5″ strips of canvas. Pad the front and back end pieces (a) and the end piece (c) so that the child will be more comfortable while lying on the frame. Cover the padding with plastic upholstery. Place the frame on top of the tub. The frame holders will just touch the sides of the tub and hold the frame motionless.

METAL CHAIR USED IN TUB

A wrought iron chair or one with a metal framework can be used as a tub chair. It gives the child support and makes it easier for the mother to get the child in and out of the tub.

If webbing is used for the seat on a wrought iron chair, measure the webbing and fold the end to make a point as described on page 73. Go over the metal framework and secure with a 1/2″ 3/16″ diameter flat head bolt and nut. Use a size 12 finishing washer so that the head is countersunk into the washer.

Cut the legs as short as desired and put a rubber tapered furniture tip on each leg to protect the tub.

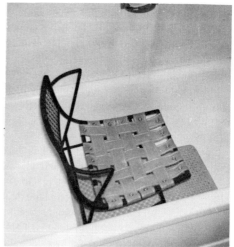

BOARD ON WHEELS

For the child who scoots around on the floor on the seat of his pants.

MATERIALS

3/4″ ply
Twelve #6 5/8″ screws and finishing washers
Sixteen #8 3/4″ screws

Casters, 4 — Plate type, ball bearing, 2″ diameter wheel — rubber tread
Polyurethane liquid plastic
Heavy weight leather

PROCEDURE

Cut a board the size that will fit the needs of your child. The one shown is 12″ x 12″. Cut a hole in the board slightly larger than the buttocks of the child. Have the saw blade angled so that the hole is beveled out. Sand and apply several coats of liquid plastic. Screw the leather on the under side of the board with 5/8″ screws and finishing washers. Screw on the casters using the #8 screws.

WEDGE BOARD

A useful aid in keeping heel cords from tightening up after surgery and adequate stretching therapy.

MATERIALS

3/4″ ply
Wilhold glue
#6 screws - 1 1/4″
Polyurethane liquid plastic

100C garnet paper
Emory cloth or traction strips —
"Scotch Tread" with adhesive back

Board
Cut 1
Width: 14 1/4″
Length: 21″

Support Stick
Cut 1
Width: 3 1/4″
Length: 19 1/2″

Board for Wedges
Cut diagonally
Width: 6 1/2″
Length: 12 1/2″

PROCEDURE

Glue the wedge-shape pieces to the sides of the board and screw into position using three 1 1/4″ screws on each side. Countersink all the screw heads. Glue and screw the support stick to the bottom inner edge of each wedge board. Sand and give several coats of liquid plastic. Glue strips of emory cloth or traction strips on the bottom of the wedges so the board cannot slip.

Using the Wedge Board

Place the board against the wall with the lower edge of the wedge board touching. The child stands on the sloping board while leaning against the wall for support. If he is facing the T.V. or a window he will be sufficiently distracted to stretch his heel cords for a longer period of time without undue complaining.

SLANT BOARD

FOR TABLE, DESK, OR WHEELCHAIR TRAY

The slant board is helpful for the child that has poor head control. The board can be set at different angles and the sliding book ledge is adjustable and removable.

MATERIALS

1/4″, 1/2″, 3/4″ ply
1 3/4″ x 3/4″ pine
1 1/4″ brads
1/4″ drill
Four 1″ and eight 1 1/2″ angle irons
Eight 1/4″ washers
Round head stove bolts — Two 2 1/4″ x 1/4″ & Two 1 1/2″ x 1/4″
#4 screws — 3/4″
#6 screws — 1/2″, 5/8″, 1″, 1 1/4″
Two 2″ butt hinges
Four 1/4″ winged nuts
Screw-Guide
Four 3″ x 3/4″ screw plates
100C garnet paper
Wilhold glue
Polyurethane liquid plastic
Electric saber saw

Sand and apply liquid plastic as you go. Use the Screw-Guide for all holes.

Slant Board
Use 1/2″ ply   Cut 1
Width: 23″
Height: 18″

Ledge
Use 1/4″ ply
Width: 1″
Length: 23″

Board B
Use 3/4″ ply   Cut 2
Width: 1 1/4″
Length: 16″

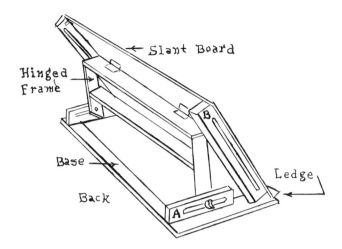

Cut the slant board. Glue the ledge to the bottom edge and screw using 3/4" #4 screws. Cut a groove in board B — 1/4" in, 1/4" from the top edge and 3/4" in from the end. Sand until smooth, rounding the top and bottom portion of the groove. See the diagram of board A on page 82.

Place the top edge flush with the top edge of the slant board. Glue into place and use a 1" angle iron with 1/2" screws on top and bottom to secure.

Hinged Frame

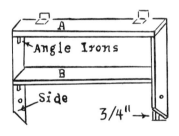

Side
Use 1 3/4" x 3/4" pine   Cut 2
Length: 7 3/4"

Support Sticks
Use 1 3/4" x 3/4" pine
Cut one 20" long (A)
Cut one 18 1/2" long (B)

Drill a 1/4" hole in the center of the side pieces 1 1/4" up from the bottom. Point each end as shown in the diagram. Glue the support stick A to the top edge of each side using brads to hold. Reenforce by screwing the 1 1/2" angle irons underneath. Do the same with support stick B which is set 3 1/2" down from A. Screw to the support stick A the 2" butt hinges 1" from each end using 5/8" screws. Be sure the pointed ends are on the same side as the hinges so that the slant board has maximum range in adjustment.

Base and Board A

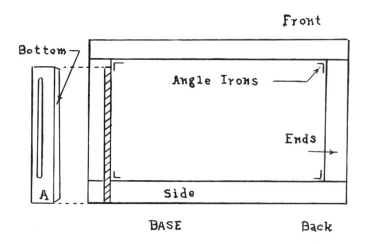

Base
Use 1 3/4″ x 3/4″ pine
Sides: Cut 2 length 23 1/4″
Ends: Cut 2 length 19 3/4″

Board A
Use 3/4″ ply   Cut 2
Width: 1 1/4″
Length: 8 1/2″

Procedure

Glue the sides of the base to the ends and secure with a 1 1/2″ angle iron in each corner. Use 5/8″ screws. For added stability, countersink the screw plates on the underside of the base and screw with 1/2″ screws. Cut a groove in board A, the same as was done on board B, page 81. Position the bottom edge of board A on the inner border of each side of the base, the ends flush with the back. Refer to the diagram above. Screw from the bottom using two 1 1/4″ screws on each board.

Sliding Book Ledge

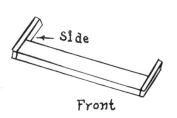

Book Ledge
Use 3/4″ ply   Cut 1
Width: 1″
Length: 23 1/8″

Side Pieces
Use 1/4″ ply   Cut 2
Width: 3/4″
Length: 2 1/4″

Glue the sides to the book ledge and secure with two #4 3/4″ screws on each end. Center and drill a 1/4″ hole 1 3/4″ from the front on each side.

Assembly

Screw the hinged frame to the slant board 4″ down from the top using 1/2″ screws. Place a 1/4″ washer on the 2 1/4″ bolt and put through the hole in the side piece of the frame and the groove in board A. Put on another washer and tighten the winged nut. The slant board can now be raised or lowered.

The book ledge is placed on the front of the slant board with the 1 1/2″ bolt going through the groove in board B and the hole in the side of the book ledge. Put a washer on both ends of the bolt and tighten the winged nut. A piece of elastic, either 1/8″ or 1/4″ wide, can be stretched across the front of the slant board, attached at the edges with tacks. This will aid in keeping a book open when standing on the book ledge.

TOOLS USED

1/4″ electric drill
28″ back saw and miter box
Screw-Guide #1465 for #6 screws
Rubber-handled screwdriver — 1/4″, 3/16″
8′ flexible metal tape
Hand saw — 10 points to the inch
T square
Tin snips
Key hole saw with different sized blades
Hammer
Pliers
8″ crescent wrench
Brace and wood bits — 1/4″ through 1″
Countersink
Metcoid 7 piece high speed drill set — 1/16″ to 1/4″
Nail setter
Hand drill
Files
Hand electric jig saw

INDEX